Also by Kleopatra Ormos, M.D.

(Available on CD)

Induction to Meditation

Journey of the Human Sculptor:
What Your Thoughts Cannot Tell You

Journey of the Human Sculptor

What Your Thoughts Cannot Tell You

Kleopatra Ormos, M.D.

SOBRAS INSTITUTE

For information please contact us at info@sobrasinstitute.com
or write to Sobras Institute, P.O. Box 647, Falmouth, MA
02541.

FIRST EDITION

Cover design by Cathi Stevenson

Library of Congress Cataloging-in-Publication Data is
available.

ISBN 0-97-53404-0-9

To all those
who graciously allowed me
to stay present
to their breathtaking growth work

Acknowledgments

My thanks and gratitude to Irene, who taught me about the importance of faith, and devotion, and that anything is possible; to Zoltan, my first mentor, who in some form is part of every word I utter; to Mariska, who demonstrated that death is no obstacle to love; to Kathy, without whose support this book would have been possible, but unlikely; to my mentors Michele Pato, M.D. and Carlos Pato, M.D. for prodding me on with loving criticism; to Nike Mandalos, Sian Roderick, and David Rowitch, M.D., Ph.D. for their thoughtful suggestions; to Katherine Scott, my copy editor, for her dependable attention to detail; to the staff at Sobras Institute, for providing me with invaluable support; to all my friends whom I can only remember with a smile; to all the mistakes I have committed; and to all my adversaries, for their honest feedback.

Contents

Symptoms 1

Inhibition - Standstill - Free Fall - Doubt - Ruminations -
Orphan of Three Parents - Anger - Solitude - Complete Betrayal -
Noise - Resentment - Losing Edge - Existential Anxiety - Resistance -
Passive Aggressiveness - Block On - Nobody Understands Me -
Denial - Fear - Emptiness - Bingeing Cycle - Longing -
Expectations - Miss You - Intellectualizing

Definitions 29

Defining - Mistakes - Genetics - Karma - Threat - Truth -
Justice - Heroes' Square - Environmental Consciousness -
Environmental Subconsciousness - Environmental
Unconsciousness - Four Fates of Nuts - Opposites -
Something - Secret - Insight - Patient

On the Couch 49

Comfort Zone - Paradox - Focus - Addiction - Facing
Addiction - The Last Moment - Knowing - Allowing - Inner
Reference Point - Fox Trot - The Table - Who Sits Behind the Table? -
Control - Power Less Struggle - Anger - Sensing - Defense - Clarity -
Unity - Projection - The Law of No Importance - Suffering -
Energy - Keepers of Difference - The Door - Resistance -
Irresistible Nonresistance - The Pen - Nut like Anybody
Else - What You Wish For - The Fork -
Guilty of Anger - Conflict

More Tools and Exercises 99

Symptoms - Balance - Center - Freedom - Power - Caution -
You Are - Mastery - Dancing

Treatments 111

Play - Awareness - Joy - Moderation - Good Relationship -
Patience - Faith - Practice

Homework and Options 121

Homework - Options

Journey of the

Human Sculptor

What Your Thoughts
Cannot Tell You

What This Book Is About

I am a psychiatrist. I am also a consultant on personal and professional development. I wrote this book for my patients.

It is often said that, over time, psychiatrists assimilate to their clients. If that is true, I did not really write this book: my patients did. More precisely, the patient in me and the psychiatrist in them wrote this book for ourselves, and I gladly share it with you.

I call this book *Journey of the Human Sculptor* to emphasize that the process I will be teaching you is similar to what a sculptor does. Michelangelo once said that when he sculpted, he simply released the form that was already in the stone. I hope that with the help of this book you will learn the skills to reveal and release universal intelligence engrained in your body to guide your personal development and healing.

"Some books are not for everybody." Although you do not need a diploma to benefit from this one, you do need an open mind about yourself and about what you can or cannot accomplish. You will not be sweet-talked into getting your butt off the couch (pun intended), and nobody is going to hold your hand through difficult, maybe painful, or half taboo topics. On the contrary, you will learn to hold your own hand through mental and emotional blocks and internal or external conflicts, which wear on you, on your health, and on your performance.

Have I mentioned that it is not a book? It is a training manual: a blue print to build reliable self-support. Anytime you feel unsure, helplessly frustrated, anxious, depressed, or enraged, the sharp reminders will quickly reconnect you with your building process. The method is described, challenged, and analyzed from various aspects throughout the manual.

Lengthy predigested materials, though at times maybe more palatable, did not prove to be helpful in getting patients off the couch. Most of them being professionals, they are also busy, and for some attention span varies from minuscule to none. Short verses and stories, metaphors, excerpts from modified therapy sessions with occasional brief explanations and mini presentations seemed to have brought them the most practical results.

These forms have proved to be highly successful tools in promoting behavioral change. I have found that

- they engage mental functions at higher levels than simple text explanations and support *transition* from passive understanding to new behavior;

- they stick in your mind and increase chances of recall *when you need it.*

It is not by accident that the Bible, the Buddhist and Taoist stories and metaphors, the Koran, and the Torah are all written in verses for ease of *repetitious* reciting, recall, and reference. I do not assume pretentious comparisons between this humble piece and the aforementioned works of great importance, but why not use, to your advantage, a *form* that has been successfully applied for hundreds and in some cases for thousands of years.

As you will see, ease of recall and repetitions are key elements of success when it comes to behavioral change and emotional development.

In most books transitions are provided; I have avoided them as much as possible to keep those "higher" mental functions engaged. Steps, logs, building plans, and instructions will be at your disposal, but you will have to pull your own mental permits and build your own bridges. The frustration you may experience about not having everything spelled out immediately as you proceed is part of the learning process to promote lasting success.

There are many ways to use the material once you understand the concept: short verses can be memorized as reminders; they are titled to provide easy reference to match your momentary mood or dilemma. You may want to ponder how metaphors, stories, and excerpts from therapy may be applicable or modified to your circumstances. Components can be used in their current order or independently and reassembled again according to your needs. It is, however, the skill to induce *experiencing* whole-body support which transcends all your thoughts or mine and which, once you learn it, will always be available to you.

Whether it relates to your inhibitions, emotional pain, work, social or private life, I invite and challenge you to build unlimited self-support, and provide for yourself in a way nobody else could provide for you.

Imagine that you are not just a builder but a sculptor chipping away at a large heavy stone blocking your path. Splinters of understanding fly off in all directions until one day, covered with dust, you face your work of art.

History of Human Sculpting and How to Apply It

The idea of writing this manual came to me many years ago, when my brother, who had been my first mentor, showed up on my doorstep with a worn suitcase and his spirit at his feet. He did not seem to have come over the ocean for a vacation. He wanted something else besides some rest for his burdened eyes over a tired smile straining across his face. But for a man who detested asking for assistance, a faint smile was the most he could churn out of himself that evening to let me know: he needed help.

The next day, when I told him over tea what I was taught during my residency, that therapy does not work with family or friends, the words burned my chin, then my chest as they trickled down from my lips. Pinned by my own beliefs and doubts at the same time, I listened to my saying to him, "I cannot be your psychiatrist," both agreeing and arguing with myself in the back seat of my mind. "To what avail were all the studies and efforts if I cannot be of any help to *him*?"

While forcing himself to understand *my* predicament, he absorbed the silent comments leaking through my eyes. Growing up with an older brother left very few hiding places for private conversations in my skull. Shared genes, adventures, and tragedies enabled him to read me like a book.

I tried to convince him that he needed to see a psychiatrist at home. "I did come to see her at home," he answered mischievously to remind me that I had come from a small forest village where people had preferred to ask for professional help (when available) from family members and friends. It had been in turn mandatory to share all possessions and knowledge to ease others' pain. Grandma, a medicine woman, had always had extra herbs, bandages, and magical stories set aside, in case someone needed but could not gather them.

I wanted a way out of my trap, so I launched my suggestion: "What I could do is challenge and guide you to explore and pinpoint inhibitions on your own and encourage you to understand how they hinder your functioning. We could use stories to model the process, through which your patterns of thinking impact on you, and observe it in action from different angles. Then, you could practice some exercises, which would promote your self-support and healing in general while decreasing your anxiety and improving your mood in particular. Even if I may not be able to help you directly, you could learn some powerful skills to help yourself."

He was game. To be perfectly safe, however, I made a thorough assessment to rule out an imminent need for medication before proceeding with the "workshop."

It pained me to think that I may not be able to accomplish much before ten days were over, nor return with him to Hungary to provide ongoing guidance. I wanted to quickly share with him the best of everything I had learned: neuroscience, psychiatry, ayurvedic and Chinese traditional medicine, Buddhism, yoga, etc.

Time, however, showed no signs of willingness to consider my lofty goals. It kept passing me by swiftly, leaving but a puny realization dangling at the bottom of the big bag I held out for help: my brother did not need either the shell nor the jargon of my education; he needed the core of its wisdom. He needed something he could take home, something he would have at his fingertips for easy access *when in need*.

He needed *skills* distilled from what was *common* in the different healing arts: the rhythm they all danced to, in their distinctive robes, the tune they all played, though in different registers, which he could resonate with in *his own voice* in order to return to well-being; in hope of what was common in *all* would be the tune his cells would recognize as familiar and find it easy to rejoin the dance alongside the universe. He also needed *the clarity* of a mentor with access to potential capacities and positioning I could not compete with: himself.

To call upon and engage his inner mentor, who by his very nature carried the common tune and rhythm in his own cells, became the goal of our work together. To experience and understand how his habitual thinking patterns, engrained in his mental circuits by his upbringing, impacted his emotional life, his biology, and imbued the context of his conflicts and temporary functional difficulties, and how he can use his body and mind to overcome them, was the focus of every story and the purpose of every exercise.

Because of his engineering background, I used many analogies from physics, which he could easily relate to. It comforted me to know that laws of nature he taught me when we were kids and I still use to help me understand human psyche, and his natural wisdom would be there for him for support - if he was willing to *allow* it - when I could not.

I used stories and metaphors with strong visuals to engage and challenge his mind, to draw analogies from and to enhance his memory. Verses and rhymes served as teasers and reminders to improve his recall. Mini presentations, which he reviewed every day, provided additional information or explanation. He practiced a simplified meditation technique I call *Induction* (see abbreviated demonstrations in *On the Couch* and an explanation in the *Appendices*) to learn to differentiate and easily switch between internal and external focus (see later) and emphasize the importance of *sensory* recall in anxiety management (see later). As caveats, simple exercises rendered complex psychological processes easier to understand without medical knowledge. I expected that his experience would be remembered longer than my words.

Working through his frustration of not knowing how to put it all together at once, before his body had a chance to *experience* a different style of processing (see later), was an important aspect of his learning. Despite his urging me to skip to the boon, I withheld some answers until *practice* itself opened his mind to associations between pieces of knowledge scattered on pages, in his body, and in time. The very synthesis, *led by* experience instead of his thinking, and burnt into the *sensory* memory of his cells, was the key to his transcending pain into skills.

I recommend that you follow a similar process to improve your chances of success. It is important that you carry out the Essential Exercises as you read them, and any time you feel stuck in your life. They will talk to you loudly and compellingly. Do not talk back; listen, feel, and watch them support and transform you.

Over the years, I modified and added to the above instruments and often reached for them, out of necessity, to aid my psychiatric and consulting practice.

They became my patients' favorite tools and reminders in their mood and anxiety management, conflict resolution, and general functioning.

I wrote the case examples to give you several ways to imagine how you could explore your inhibitions, or inquire about your anxiety, and at the same time, experiment with using *Induction* on your own. All cases are based on real-life examples, modified only to protect patients' identity. Practice *Induction* as often as you can. It is the most essential exercise and the foundation of the concept I share with you in this manual.

The complete program includes, among others, lifestyle changes that favor natural rhythms and foods, timing of exercise and water intake, building a supportive external environment, and healing injuries. These topics will be handled in detail in another book currently under preparation. To best benefit from the sequel, however, applied knowledge of the contents of this manual is indispensable.

After my brother returned to Hungary and was functioning well, he coined the term "human sculpting" to describe what I was doing. Since it was clear to me that I could not have accomplished much without his *becoming* the Sculptor himself, I teased him: "If that is true, what are you now, a human or a sculpture?" I asked, rubbing my hands together mischievously, assuming that I had pinned him down. I was wrong, for he replied: "I am whatever I *experience* when I choose to apply the skills I learned from you."

Sometimes, I still ponder whether he was grinning or gloating after we hung up. You just never know with siblings . . .

*Your
past and your future
will remain your thoughts;
reality is
what you practice.
This moment is your conscience:
it reflects what you
practice.*

Introduction

However annoying or uncomfortable you find your problems to be, they are your private studios. They dare you to express your creativity as you respond to challenges. They appear as distinctive fragments of all sizes and colors, but together they tell a story: your story. Your mind fuses them into patterns, which shape your experience, and solidifies them in hard structures of beliefs on who you are and what the world is like.

Solutions are not just carefully thought out concepts but also living processes of your entire organism in concert with your environment. Problem solving is not a monopoly of your thinking. It is engrained in your body just as much as in your mind and is activated through your experience.

The seat of your thoughts is in the so-called gray matter, which is the outermost layer of your brain. This layer is also the seat of concepts, logic, and analysis and is among the most sophisticated and most recent manifestations of universal intelligence in the history of the Earth's development. Therefore, you have good reason to be proud of your thoughts.

Besides unquestionable beauty and success, however, thoughts on Earth also have a track record of causing unbearable disaster and suffering. Thinking is a quick and sensitive tool but one with an enormous margin of error. When not balanced by ancient more accurate mechanisms in your system, dysfunction or destruction is unavoidable. These ancient mechanisms are orchestrated from deeper and developmentally older parts of your brain, which also house emotions and sensing.

Human Sculpting is about balance, harmony, and synergy between developmentally older and younger sections of your brain to bring about your best performance. It is beyond beauty, success, suffering, or survival. It is beyond logic or science or free association of poetry. For it is an art: your art of personal transformation and healing.

Symptoms

Inhibition

[Recipe]

Take a random thought.
Marinate it in a quart of your parents' anxiety
with a pinch of your grandparents' fear, and
ruminate them over medium frustration
stirring constantly.
Stays fresh without refrigeration.

Standstill

When a moment feels stale, tiresome, or stifling,
your trip has been halted:
You refuse to move on to the next moment.

Free Fall

You split reality
into good and bad
and fall
into the gap trap.

Doubt

You discount infinity
and yourself in its core
until everything is
sold out.

Ruminations

First you think,
then you doubt,
then you think and doubt.

Orphan of Three Parents

One has been absent in body;
the other is absent-minded;
the third abandons you daily.

Anger

You are stuck in anger
when you have difficulties
feeling angry,
because you are distracted
by *thoughts* of blame.

Solitude

Among many thoughts,
a single emotion finds you alone.

Complete Betrayal

Even your anger
leaves you.

Noise . . .

. . . is the only
company
of the lonely.

Resentment . . .

. . . is your edge
without a sword,
your nausea without
the catharsis of puking,
your war without battles:
a silent annihilation of yourself.

Losing Edge

A tone with sharp edges
cuts deepest into your throat,
where it is born.
Righteousness or guilt in its wake
upsets your stomach, and the
disturbed digestion
weakens your heart.

Existential Anxiety

Your soul exposed to your mind.

Resistance

The more you resist,
the more the universe insists.

Passive Agressiveness

In a universe where
everything is in constant transformation,
passivity requires active participation.

Block On

Memory of the last moment
blocks your full participation
in this moment.
What you hold on to
blocks the flow of receiving
and giving.
Images block your vision.
Who you think you are
blocks your becoming . . .

Nobody Understands Me

Maybe they do.
As humans, they share
ninety-nine percent
of your genes.

So, the other
is more like your brother,
or your sister,
or your other half...
in fact, a little less
than both your halves.

They, too, mortgage
ninety-nine percent
of their thoughts
from the collective unconscious,
which makes them
potentially intimate
with anybody who moves.

They cannot
but understand you,
provided that
they understand themselves.
Do you understand me?

Denial . . .

. . . sleeps with your evidence.

Fear . . .

. . . is your denial of responsibility.
You fear the world,
because you doubt yourself.

As if you were a short circuit
without real connection to
the powers
that created you.

As if you were not a part of
threatening situations,
just as lightning is
part of thunderstorms.

When you are afraid,
you focus on
what seems
to come at you,
and forget what
you bring to the circumstances.

Emptiness . . .

. . . is a hole
in your Whole
to sneak out.

Bingeing Cycle

Craving the future,
you devour the past.
Now, you are fed up.
Down you go.

Longing

The more you long for
something,
the less you connect with
the whole.

Expectations

You give and expect;
therefore you do not give:
you pay for your wish
to receive.

Miss You

Who you think I am
does not allow you
to see *me*.
I am sorry
we have never met.

Intellectualizing

When you think you know yourself,
you do not know yourself:
you think.
When you think you trust yourself,
you do not trust yourself:
you think.
You think you are too vulnerable
to feel.

Definitions

Defining . . .

. . . confines you
to your definitions.

Mistakes . . .

. . . are your approximations
of perfection.

Genetics

Your father procrastinated.
Your mother procrastinated.

You are procrastinated.

Karma

We are conquerors not
because we are better at detecting threat but
because we are better at creating it.

In our wake,
the wounded collective memory of the world
scars our image on the face of the universe.

Threat . . .

. . . is rarely a surprise.
It is the consequence of a gradual
selective reduction to the
only path that
the circumstances
and your previous actions
allow.

Truth . . .

. . . prevails over lies
in a world without unity.

Justice . . .

. . . just
adjusts.

Heroes' Square

Capture O'Judgment
Puking De Blame
Depleted Bye Victory
Rest In Peace

Environmental Consciousness

History recycles.

Environmental Subconsciousness

History recycles.
You argue.

Environmental Unconsciousness

History recycles.
You argue.
You are being recycled.

Four Fates of Nuts

Sprouting
self-sustaining
increasing integrity

Vegetating
be sustained
decreasing integrity

Rotting
not sustained
losing integrity

Being Eaten
sustaining others
be integrated

Opposites

"Nothing" is not the opposite of "everything".
The opposite of "everything" is "something".

Something

Secret . . .

. . . is what you are not
ready to understand.

Insight . . .

. . . which sprouts
between your truth
and a hard place,
is rarely enough.

It may trigger
your change,
yet without action,
remains mere thought
and becomes your obstacle.

Patient . . .

. . . is a person
who hangs in there until
healing finally takes place,
despite treatment.

On the Couch

Comfort Zone

Are you sure
you are ready to handle
the implications of awareness?
Or are you still too weak
to assume your nature?

Awareness is powerful . . .
power comes with *responsibility* . . .
of those who understand . . .
of those who can . . .
under any circumstances.

Are you *really*
ready to relinquish
your claim to helplessness,
shame, and doubt?

Paradox

He is a single, dynamic, very accomplished business executive with legs and thoughts longer than the couch.

"This is my paradox:" he launches ahead. "On the one hand, I understand that this moment *is* because the universe is. On the other hand, I know that there is no such thing as a moment. It is a concept, an arbitrarily frozen constellation of my thoughts, only a *picture* of the never-ceasing transformations of information, energy, and matter. Am I driving myself crazy?"

"Do you feel crazy?" I ask him instead of answering.

"At times when I mull over such questions in order to understand something and I get myself even more confused. Do you understand my paradox?"

"Let me summarize it, and correct me if I am wrong. You describe a split view of unity. Unity is indivisible, but when you think, you can only concentrate on one of its aspects at a time. You seem to have difficulty dealing with *everything*."

"It is too big for me . . . but I understand that narrowing my vision to a pinpoint does not mean that there is a point, or that the many points I have looked at are the building points of unity."

"What if every point is unity? What if every point is whole within itself, and every point is the whole? In a hologram, for instance, the entire picture can be reconstituted from its fragment. The larger the fragment the more detailed the picture is going to be, but the picture itself does not change. The fragment *is* the picture. They are of the same nature. It seems to me that you try to *solve* the paradox because you do not dare to *enter* it."

I pause. He grins.

"I am seduced by unity," he admits.

"But you do not dare to admit that it is your nature and, therefore, ignoring it is reckless endangerment."

"If it is my nature then entering it is incest!"

He leans forward and spews at me as if he was vomiting up a secret. I stay measured in my reply.

"You look upset."

He ignores me and directs his gaze out the window. I rest mine on him, worried that he may loose balance if I give him another push. I wait patiently until his mind returns to the room and feels comfortable enough to speak.

"Do you believe in God?" he asks almost whispering.

"Is God important to you?"

"I do not know much about Him or Her, but when I lie sleeplessly at night, it is so loud in my head that I almost wonder if God may hear my thoughts."

"About?"

He looks down at his hands, then at the floor in front of his feet. I ask him again.

"Is it hard to say?"

He looks at me for a moment, then his eyes seek refuge on the floor again as if down below is the only safe place. He does not look up when he utters his words.

"Am I everything, am I unity, am I the universe?"

We sit together in silence for a few moments before I address him quietly.

"What do you feel right now?"

"Shame."

"Of what?"

"Of daring to assume such a preposterous stance. I am a little scared, too, that I lost my mind."

"What do you see in your mind's eye?"

"I am sitting in a vacuum as the roaring laughter of people looking at me with pity abates when they get up and go."

"Do they answer you?"

"There is no answer . . . the questions are gone, too . . . "

He nervously scratches his thighs with his thumbs.

"Even the moment deserts me," he adds.

I watch him struggle with tears. He finally surrenders to crying gently without a sob. I get up and fetch him a Kleenex box. He accepts it and pulls out a couple of tissues to dry his face. I resume my place and wait until he settles before going on.

"What do you feel?"

"Lonely . . . sad," he answers.

"Is it okay to close your eyes and allow yourself to feel sad and lonely for a little longer?"

He nods and shuts his eyes.

"Where do you feel sad?" I ask.

"In my chest."

We sit. I focus on sensing my chest before I continue.

"Now, become aware of your fingertips . . ." I say, and in support, I also focus on my fingertips. "What do you feel?"

"Throbbing in my fingertips," he answers.

I lead him through a series of suggestions, pausing for a few seconds between each sentence.

"Become aware of your toes . . . There is no need to expect anything special; just feel what it feels like to have toes . . . sense them from the inside . . . when you are able to feel your toes, sense your fingertips and toes *at the same time* . . . carry this sensation all the way up your leg . . . through your pelvis and belly . . . through your chest and throat . . . to your head, and sense your head . . . feel your head . . . fingertips . . . and toes . . . *at the same time* . . . notice what your body *feels* like when you feel your head . . . fingertips . . . and toes . . . *at the same time* . . . what do you feel?"

"Relaxed . . . ripples of tiny waves throughout my body . . . it is very pleasant."

"If the rate of your thoughts was at one hundred percent before we started the exercise, what percentage would you assign to their rate when you felt your head, fingertips, and toes at the same time?"

"About ten percent."

"Do you feel a need for a question right now?"

"No."

"For answers?"

"No."

A truck passes by in the street, below the office windows. He lies comfortably with his eyes shut as if he did not hear the noise.

"Do the sounds from the street bother you?" I ask.

"No. I feel them, rather than I hear them," he answers calmly.

"Feel them?"

"As if they entered me through my skin and with my breath . . ."

"Let them flush through your muscles and your bones . . . keep feeling your head . . . fingertips . . . and toes . . . and open your eyes. Notice a momentary distraction from sensing your body . . . let it happen . . . sense your head, fingertips, and toes *at the same time* . . . and look at an object in front of you without naming or describing it . . . just *see* it."

He fixes his gaze at the computer screen on my desk.

"What do you feel?" I ask him.

"As if it were in continuity with me."

"What is the rate of your thoughts in this moment?"

"About the same . . . maybe less . . ."

"How do you feel?"

"Very relaxed . . . and aware."

"Where do you feel aware?"

"Inside . . ."

"Inside the paradox?"

Focus

When you focus on sensing your body, the rate of your thoughts decreases. When you think about an issue, your general awareness of physical sensations lessens. Neuroscience calls this phenomenon "gating."

Although gating limits how much information you can process at once, you can also play it as a dirty little trick to sneak by your gloomy thoughts without waking up the sleeping lions. As long as you focus on experiencing a sensation in your body, the entry of your thoughts through the gate will be thwarted: physical sensations will pin you to this moment, preventing any slipping into the pain of the past or into the anxiety of the future.

Resisting does not work. If you fight, judge, or try to get rid of any disturbing thoughts, you focus your attention on *them* and facilitate their entry through the gate. Your experience will reflect *where* your focus hangs out, not *what* you wish. You will keep hurting until you are willing to drop what you long for and, for the time being, refocus on what you *are*. "What you are" is what you *sense* in your body in this moment. The rest is your story.

Addiction

[A Testimony]

I used to believe that I could think my way through life. Now, it is clear that I can think my way only through thoughts. I wake up with them and hold them very close until I fall asleep in the evening. We think of each other many times a day. In fact, there are thoughts I have thought every day since I can remember. They lounge in my body, stand between me and whom I may be talking to, and fall into my lunch bowl . . . I see the future through their eyes. I see and hear them anywhere I look. I see them, not what I am looking at.

I had never thought of my thinking as a liability. It worked for me in school. I was rewarded for remembering and thinking other people's thoughts and concepts. Since I never got praised for remembering feeling good, I learned to think very well. There is just so much more I can accomplish with thinking . . . except feeling. I was taught that feelings happen. I was also taught that I can make things happen if I work hard.

So I worked very hard and did a lot of thinking to increase my chances of feeling well one day. I thought a lot about feeling. The more I thought, the less I felt. One day I realized I was addicted: I could not be without my thoughts any more, and it made me feel lousy. I joined Thinkers Anonymous.

I attend regularly. I also meditate. My thoughts meditate with me. They chant loud comments on what I do. I feel haunted and stifled. I watch people to see if they have similar problems and how they may deal with them. I listen to them: they talk about their . . . thoughts!

I feel deeply hurt and betrayed. I have thought that my thoughts and I were unique for each other . . . Now I know that they are the prostitutes of all the people, maybe even of animals. We frequent the same thoughts over and over again.

I am so shattered by this realization that I cannot think for a little while. Thoughtless, I float in the sensations of my body. To my surprise, I feel relaxed, refreshed, and energized. Without the constant noise in my head, I am confronted with sudden clarity: "Thoughts I stick to will stick to me and make me stuck."

Facing Addiction

Addiction is hard to kick, and
you are not trained as a warrior to tackle
what brought empires down
before you.

But you have choices.
You are free to exit the moment
your thoughts belong to.

Every new instant
has a clean slate
until you contaminate it
with your memory.

Every new instant is
your chance to focus
on something else,
on all else,
on everything.

When you think it is "impossible" or
you "cannot do this",
they are your thoughts, too, which
you have learned, and
you are conditioned to think.
They, too, belong to a moment
that will end
in this instant.

The Last Moment . . .

. . . is dead;
gently
move on.

Knowing

Dear John,

You stock up on the particulars of what has happened, and savoring them, you wonder why you relive past events and experiences. As if it were me, not you, inflicted with what Freud called repetition compulsion.

Endless inner talk shows and commentaries consume most of your attention and energy. A captive fan of your memories' reruns, you become your thoughts by habit; I become them by default.

I have no agenda of my own; you do. I am invoked. Rather like light, which is both wave and particle, I am energy, matter, or an event, depending on what circumstances call for.

For you, my dear, I manifest according to what you incite me to be by your so-called "knowing." When you *know*, I become *what* you know. When you doubt, I become your doubt. When you doubt that anything is possible anytime, you exclude the possibility that I can be "anything" for you. And since you do not know everything, dear John, I cannot become "everything" for you. When you think you know, you interfere with infinity to unfold with clarity for you, and I become your mistake.

When you suspend knowing, however, you *allow* the processes of *becoming* in its entirety. Your openness will invite and your *experience* will enable me to become anything and everything for you.

Love,
Reality

Allowing . . .

. . . not knowing,
is the matrix of
infinite becoming.

Inner Reference Point

[A Journal Entry]

Inner reference point is the *process* of sensing. Being centered in my inner reference point does not equal selfishness or being right. The latter are products of thinking. When I am connected to my inner reference point, I am aware of the physical sensations in my body. I do not recall my memory of the past or dreams of the future, and I do not define, name, compare, or label what I feel. I engage both my body and my mind in sensing the entirety of *this* moment.

I experience the environment *through* my body, as if there were no separation between me, the objects I see, the sounds I hear, and the temperature I feel. I do not hear the birds sing; I sense the melody of their songs in the vibrations of my body. I do not see them, I sense their flight in my muscles, and I absorb their colors. I feel them as I feel my fingertips. I am relaxed and content. I feel joy. I sense it in my body as energy.

When thoughts resurface in my mind, my focus wanders to them as if they were magnets, and I disconnect from sensing. I focus on what they reflect: outside reference points. Though my thoughts seem to be mine, they are in fact the products of a life-long conditioning process by my environment.

I no longer absorb the colors, but name them. I do not feel the temperature in my bones, but determine the degrees. I do not sense the flight of birds, I define their speed, distance, and direction, and I remember that cormorants notoriously soil my boat. I do not feel the direct connection with my body, and I do not connect with people with whom I interact, because my thoughts wedge between us. I *notice* the tension in my neck, *but I do not* stop the commentaries in my mind in order to *sense* the pain. I am afraid of it, and I avoid it, and in my absence it worsens.

I *know* what is happening, which *prevents me from experiencing* it. Knowing, however, is a poor substitute for *feeling joy and energy*. As if my thoughts cut me off from my energy source, the more I think, the more disconnected I feel. I am anxious and fearful. My muscles tense up. I try to think positively, but I do not believe myself. When I attempt to discard my thoughts, they flood my mind. The more I push them away, the more they hang on to me.

When I stop trying, I experience a moment of relief. At last, I remember to check in with my fingertips. I feel them together with my toes and my head, all at the same time. In a split second, I dissolve in the energy of my body. It is impossible to describe fully what I feel even if I cared to resuscitate my thoughts, which have suddenly collapsed. The quick onset of comfort, calmness, and vibrating energy in my body convinces me that I do not *need* words to feel joy.

A fleeting doubt sneaks in to constrict my chest for a moment: "Sensing my fingertips cannot solve my problems! It only serves as a distraction." I look the intruder straight in the eye: "No doubt. I use the *exercise* of sensing to remind me that problems are but distractions from joy."

Fox Trot

While I take a brief pause to drink some water, she lowers her head onto her left shoulder and bathes her face in the sun, which gleams through the window. Then, she leans over the armrest of her chair and looks down onto my backyard, carefully surveying the action around the bird feeders.

"Do you remember the fox you saw in my yard during last session?" I ask her.

"Yes," she answers without quitting what she was doing, as if not wanting to miss a beat of bird news.

"How did you know it was a fox?" I prod as insidiously as I can manage.

She turns away from the window, repositions herself in her seat, and looks at me curiously.

" I just knew it . . . but then . . . I was wondering if it was a German shepherd."

"You were wondering . . ." I repeat her words, acknowledging what I heard.

"Well, you know, most of her body was behind a tree . . . and a German shepherd can also have a rusty bushy tail.

"Have you noticed any difference between your first impression and the second time around?"

"The first was instantaneous . . . the second took some while."

"The wondering?"

"The thinking," she replies, grinning.

"*How* did you know it was a fox the first time . . . without thinking?"

"I just knew".

"How?"

"I don't know . . . as if I knew and sensed it at the same time . . ."

"Sensed *it*?"

"I mean sensed her."

"The fox?"

"Must have been . . . maybe I saw her for a split second before she slipped behind the tree trunk. I must have recognized the colors and the shape; otherwise, I could not have known . . . Is that right? But it was more than that . . ."

I wait.

"I felt like I knew . . . " she adds.

"You *felt* like you knew . . . "

63

"It is hard to explain . . . I sort of knew with my whole body in an instant, not just with my thinking . . . it was not an isolated operation . . . although thinking must have been part of it . . . but it was just a part, nothing more . . . yes . . . thinking was just a part of something bigger . . . more complete . . . something that did not exclude my body . . . or the fox or the connection I felt between us . . . if it makes any sense."

"Does it make any sense to you?"

"Yes, I remember the experience."

"The *experience*?"

"Yes."

"Let me summarize what I heard you say: when you were in the analyzing mode, you were thinking of *it* instead of sensing-knowing *her*."

"That is a good way of putting it, I can resonate with *her*."

I cannot help but giggle at her clever joke.

She joins me and adds: "Again, it may sound silly, but instantaneously, I sort of knew *and* sensed her at the same time."

"Where did you know and sense her?

"Inside me . . ."

"Inside you . . . what kind of evidence is that?"

"None, I guess . . ."

"You trusted your inside *without evidence*?"

"I did not think to doubt it . . . it happened so quickly . . . I did not think at all at first."

"So, when did you start doubting yourself?"

"When I asked myself if it was a German shepherd."

"When you asked yourself?"

"Yes."

"Ask and you shall doubt . . . is that what you are saying?

"You make me."

"Do not let *me* make you do anything, let alone doubt *yourself*. Let's review it all in slow motion again: start from when you knew it was a fox. Then what happened?"

"Then I started to think . . . that maybe . . . "

"You said *think* and *maybe* . . . is that correct?"

"Yes."

I wait.

"Well . . . I guess you are right . . . " she says.

"I did not say I was, but do you *think* I did?"

"I guess." She squirms on her chair.

"Correct me if I am wrong: I hear you say that you started to doubt yourself when you started to think."

"I'm afraid, that is correct."

"From what you have said, I also understand that you did not doubt yourself when you had no time to think."

"That sounds disturbing."

"Is that what you think?"

"Yes."

"Do you *feel* disturbed?"

"And uncomfortable . . . Where is this leading to?"

"Wherever *thinking* takes us down the path of logic in search of reason and evidence. So far we have only found doubt, disturbance, discomfort . . . "

"I want to stop."

"Stop thinking?"

"You have it."

"Okay. Close your eyes, please."

We take a couple of minutes to induce a quick guided shift of focus from thoughts to physical sensations in her body. Starting with concentrating on feeling her fingertips, then her toes, then her head, she induces whole-body sensation by feeling the separate components *all at the same time*. In support, I complete the exercise simultaneously. Then, while maintaining my focus on sensing my body, I direct her to do the same *as* she recalls feeling connection with the fox.

" . . . just the way you did the very first time . . . can you sense her?"

"Yes," she answers.

I pause before each question that ensue.

"Can you see the colors of her tail without naming or analyzing them?"

"Vividly."

"Does *seeing* her colors prevent you from *feeling* her?"

"No."

"Can you feel her right now?

"Yes."

"Where?"

"Inside me."

"Are you *thinking* of her?"

"No."

"Do you see the colors of her tail nevertheless?"

"Yes."

"Keep feeling her. Are you thinking of anything?"

"No."

"Are you doubting yourself?"

"No."

"Are you feeling disturbed or uncomfortable?"
"No."
"What do you feel?"
"My body . . . the fox . . . relaxed."
"Do you feel a connection with the fox?"
"Yes."
"Does it feel good?"
"Very special . . . "
"Without evidence?"

The Table

[An Essential Exercise]

Sit in front of your desk and place your hands on its flat surface.

Feel its smoothness as you move your palms on it. Feel its temperature, and sense its hardness. See its colors.

Remove your hands and turn away from the table.

How sure are you that when you return to it in a couple of minutes it will have the same texture, hardness, temperature, and color?

How about in a week, or a year from now?

How much do you trust that your experience is reliably reproducible?

Who Sits Behind the Table?

She slowly opens her eyes after completing "The Table" exercise.

"What is your hunch, will the texture and the temperature of the table feel the same to you if you replace your hands on it in two minutes?" I ask.

"Yes," she answers.

"Will the color look the same?"

"Yes."

"How about in a week or in a year?"

"The same."

"How sure are you?"

"Pretty sure . . . "

I take a few moments to rest my expressionless eyes on her until she starts to squirm on the chair. Then I break the silence:

"How sure are you that your experience is reliably reproducible?"

" Well, if I take every possible scenario into account, lots of things can happen . . . "

"For instance?"

"Something could fall on the table and break it."

"A meteor?" I ask.

She laughs.

"How often has that happened to you?" I continue.

"You know what I mean . . ." she says.

"Are you asking me if I could reliably reproduce in *my* head the thought *you* just had?"

"No . . . I meant that I only know what I feel in this moment, I cannot predict the future."

"But you did predict that lots of things *can* happen, and it made you unsure."

"That is true."

"So, who was sure a little while ago that the texture and the temperature of the table would feel the same and its color would look the same in two minutes, in a week, or in a year?"

"I was sure.

"How is that possible?"

She ponders.

"I am not sure . . . " she admits.

"I am not sure, either . . . but I noticed that you showered me with lots of words when the meteor fell . . . yet you were very frugal with words right after the exercise. What happened?"

She ponders again.

"After the exercise I still saw the color vividly and felt the sensations in my hands."

"And that made you sure?"

"Yes."

"So you felt the sensations in your hands, and saw the color . . . What did you see later, when your words came in rapid succession?"

"I suddenly saw in my imagination all the different scenarios that could happen . . . "

"What is the chance that they would?"

"Slim."

"For that slim chance you abandoned your sureness?"

Control

Your thoughts are weightless. They can change shape, size, and content, or spin out of control and space in a split second. When you project your fearful images onto others, subtly or overtly, you demand your environment to adjust in order to relieve *your* anxiety.

On the other hand, predictability lends a calming sense to physical sensations. There is a good chance that you will find your desk smooth, cool, and flat in five minutes or even five months later. Without doubting the table or yourself, when you sense, you *trust* that your experience is reproducible.

Staying connected to your body-sense keeps you *predictably* available to support and soothe yourself. When you are connected, there is no need to control the environment to decrease your anxiety.

Power Less Struggle

[A Journal Entry]

Not until I started to climb the stairs to the shower did I notice that I was shaking. My bones, stuck in some fine but pervasive tremor, provided no solid structure for my muscles. Groundless, I vacillated between surrendering to the faint voice of reason and mercy to sit down and the numbing fear of exploding if I did, if I forfeited the protection of measured continuous action. On borrowed strength I entered the bathroom, turned on the shower, undressed, and stepped into the tub.

The warmth of the thousands of prodding water drops infiltrated my skin and gently corralled my soul into their pool. Defenseless, I watched the dawn penetrate the many layers of darkness to stain me in the tub. By the time the night evaporated from the bathroom floor, the trembling had abated.

Calmer, I thought I could afford to review what had happened. But recalling the first fragment of memory sent a chilling shiver through my veins. I backed off and idled in measured, continuous movements.

No motion was too simple to rediscover the joy of mastery and control again: drying off, hanging up the towel. No clothes were too familiar to welcome a homey feeling in their shelter.

Finally, I made it to my office. I sank into my chair as if to buckle in and turn the ignition on to make the move to understand.

A stifling sensation in my chest, which I could neither throw up nor digest, grew as you shrank in the rearview mirror. I was distancing myself from you with thousands of angers per second.

"Why did you throw your birthday present from me into the dirt? That hurt. You also ignored my request about . . . oh, well . . . yes, I'll live . . . for what was worse: you left me for your self-blame when I needed your arms to say you were sorry. I felt I was living our marriage alone as you were off with your self-slut again."

My thoughts were racing faster than light, leaving me in the darkness of rage of the abandoned, until finally my body arrested them for speeding. Having been placed under the probation of measured, continuous, simple activity again, my thoughts settled down enough to be able to collaborate with the rest of me. I fumbled with the mindless physical tasks of cleaning my desk, rearranging the furniture. It worked.

The noise in my head abated. I waited. I rested. I peered into the silence. In the distance I thought I had seen something on the ground. I did not dare to move closer to see clearly. I was afraid it was you — or worse, your body lying on the ground run over and slain by my thoughts.

"What authority did my thoughts have to condemn me to deny you? What right did they have to keep me a prisoner of my own rules? What did I gain from disconnecting myself from your realness?

You did not fail me. I failed to stay present when you left."

Anger

[A Reminder]

You are stuck in anger
when you have difficulties
feeling angry,
because you are distracted
by *thoughts* of blame.

Sensing

When you are connected to your inner reference point, you *sense* your presence in the world. You do not think of it, or of yourself. You *experience* what it feels like to have a body, to breathe, to be able to move, feel, and interact. You identify with the *energy* of sensations and emotions, not with their meaning.

Sensing is your tool to smoothly tune into the field you *share*, rather than the one you *have*. You understand what you experience by participation, not by judgment. You *hold* and sense the world, instead of poking it with your thoughts, then exposing your body to their by-products.

Sensing functions as a valve to avoid blockages in your energy flow. Anger, fear, anxiety, or suffering warn you that valve functions are down, and free-flow has been disrupted: somewhere in your system, there is an obstruction in the form of a *sense*less thought.

Defense . . .

. . . is a breakthrough of clarity,
not anger.
It is harmonious action,
not reaction.
It is synchronizing,
not an attempt
to halt or go against force
or motion.

Defense is not a counterattack.
On the contrary,
it is action in concert
with the circumstances
in order to ease,
not increase,
the tension.

Judging or blaming will
disconnect and weaken you.
You must absorb and
join the energy flow of
the *entire* moment,
even if it seems scary,
unattractive, or
counterintuitive
at first.

For it is the direct contact
achieved by
unconditional understanding
that best positions you
for making
a *lasting* change.

Clarity . . .

. . . is the *experience* of unity,
from which you disconnect
the moment
you judge or blame.

Clarity is the *freeflow* of
energy and information.
It is *connection*, which renders
judging and blaming unnecessary.

It is the unmistakable
understanding that
you are not separate from
what you see or experience:

You cannot exclude
what you hate, or reject,
admire, or envy,
just as the universe
does not exclude you when
you are hateful, rejecting,
amorous, or envious.

Unity . . .

. . . makes it difficult to blame or
hide behind ignorance
and incapacitation.

Your challenge is
to experience unity *before*
being condemned to it.

Projection

Value and Nonsense live in a rocky relationship. They both feel unhappy and turn to Reason for advice: "We are attracted or repulsed, angry or elated, but never just content."

Nonsense longs for Value's beauty, and it pains him to feel separate. Other times, he is annoyed: "She is unreal!" Reason intervenes: "How could you miss her if she were not real?"

Value thinks that Nonsense is a nuisance; and he is noisy, too. She can barely hear her thoughts when he is around. She resents him and doubts herself, but she listens to Reason: "If he were not important to you, how could he make you *so* angry?"

The ebb and flow of their emotions erode the moments and the years. At last, they feel fine. As Nonsense looses his sight, and Value grows deaf, they no longer need Reason.

The Law of No Importance

Nothing is important. Everything *is,* and everything is proportionate to the whole. "Important" is but a flag to alert you that you are in the process of applying meaning and distorting something into what it is not.

Its possible Latin origin *importo,* which translates as "carry in," warns you: you drag meaning and importance with you like dead carcasses wherever you go in your mind, mostly to the past and the future. It is not until you trip over something meaningless and unimportant, blocked out of your vision, that you may realize you have been living in the unreal: objects appear larger than they are.

You stifle moments with meaning and importance. Taken out of *their* context, distorted into labels and thought fragments, they die well before you swallow them into your memory.

You, too, become a fragment when your thoughts distract you from the nature of this moment, which is whole without meaning or importance. "Everything" is reduced to meaning, when you disconnect from the freshness and wholeness of this instance.

This moment is the only living cell. This untagged, undistorted, nonexclusive, vibrating moment in constant transformation is you. Your thoughts are only dots on the pegboard.

Suffering

You suffer when you *think* of the loss you experience. More precisely, you do not experience, because your focus is glued to your thoughts. A splinter of everything becomes your reality in your mind, and in this process you become a splinter of yourself. You suffer from *disapproval* of your experience.

You suffer from threat of diminishing comfort, happiness, or survival, and forget that suffering is survivors' entitlement as well as luxury. So are comfort and balance when you *choose to sense* them in your body. But full-time suffering does not allow for sensing. In this monopoly lies the power of suffering.

Pain lessens when you sense it directly without the *meaning* of loss. Sorrow is temporary when you are willing to feel it without the distortions of your interpretation. When you choose to experience pain and sorrow as purely physical sensations in your body, there will be neither time nor opportunity for suffering.

Energy

When your thoughts label
emotions as "negative,"
you want to avoid
or get rid of them.

As you negate "them,"
you *negate* a part of yourself,
your energy,
and with time you will feel
depleted and exhausted.

When you experience emotions
purely on an energetic level,
every feeling, every interaction
will empower and energize you.

Emotions and sensations,
be they anger, pain, or joy,
will be your living reminder
of the *power* you share:

a taste of the *energy*
and the *intelligence*
that maintain life,
against all odds,
on Earth.

Keepers Of Difference

After an intermediate-level exercise of *Induction*, I asked him to look at me. When he finally did, his eyes twinkled from the gorge of his wrinkles carved by countless years at sea.

"What was your experience?" I inquired.

"I was surprised how easy it was today to stay with sensing my fingertips, toes, and head and at the same time think my thoughts and feel the emotions they stirred up. I felt the passion of my anger in my body . . . and, at the same time, the calming sensation of energy in my fingertips and toes and then all over in my body . . ."

"Were you able to sense the energy of your emotions in your body *as* you were thinking?"

"Yes."

"Were you able to shift your focus easily between your thoughts, the energy of your emotions, and sensing your fingertips, toes, and head?"

"Yes . . . easily, but not quite smoothly."

"What did you experience?"

"A glitch between the energy of emotions and the energy of feeling my fingertips and toes."

"Can you tell me more?"

"Anger felt almost like a demonic energy . . . while during *Induction* I always feel some sort of clean energy."

"Clean?"

"Well, until this exercise, I have never really labeled it clean. I have only noticed the difference today . . . when I felt the two different types of energy, one after another . . . "

"What do you make of it?"

"I do not know . . . "

"Do you remember the thoughts attached to the 'demonic type' energy you have experienced today?"

"Yes, I remember them very well."

"Were you thinking them when you felt that type of energy?"

"Yes."

"Do you remember the thoughts attached to your fingertips and toes?"

He laughs. "Usually there aren't any," he says.

"So what was the difference between the two energies?"

The Door

[An Essential Exercise]

Stand two feet away from a shut solid door. Place both your hands on it at shoulder level. Start pushing the door.
Notice the resistance it offers to your palms.

Push *harder*.
Notice what happens to the resistance. Does it decrease, increase, or stay the same?
Do not respond. Knowing is not enough.

Feel your answers in your palms, then let go of the door.
What happened to the resistance? Is there a difference?
If there is, *feel* it.

Place your hands in the same position again, and this time push as hard as you can. Push until you feel *pain* in your arms or between your shoulder blades.
Notice the relationship between pushing and hurting.

Let go of the door, and feel your body.
What happened to the pain?

Let your body do all the talking. It will hold on to your answers much longer than your thoughts and remind you much sooner *when you need* to remember.

If you do this exercise only in your head right now, and not at the door, you are missing the point and an opportunity to make a change. Maybe this is how you have missed many other points and opportunities in your life. *Knowing the answers is not enough.* " It may trigger your change, yet without action, remains mere thought and becomes your obstacle."

So please understand and respect your resistance, then without belittling it, *move through* its cracks. Get up . . . and go to the door before you move on to the next page. You will not regret it. The rest of the manual assumes your *experiencing* this exercise, which builds your skills to become succsessful in whatever you undertake.

Resistance

[A Reminder]

The more you resist,
the more the universe insists.

Irresistible Nonresistance

Do not *try* to push any thoughts away, because their resistance will always match your effort. They are yours, but they are not everything, so treat them accordingly. Let them come and stay as they please, and refocus on sensing your body. Leave all doors and windows open and they shall leave just as they came.

Do not *try* to get rid of your doubts and judgments. They are family as well as your inheritance. Bow to them, when they enter the room without knocking, and watch them lurk in the corner for a while until you recognize them all. When your eyes meet theirs, wink and refocus on sensing your body. They will not stick around without you as a captive audience.

When you feel sad or angry, do not *try* to think positively, "snap out of it," or judge how you feel. It can be a fatal mistake to ignore your emotions or insult their intelligence. Emotions are true warriors. They carry immense energy. But they are also big babies. All they want is to be seen, acknowledged, and cuddled. They like to feel close and intimate, so provide both for them. But do not listen to their words or suggestions, and do not become their stage or sounding board.

Instead, breathe them in, absorb them through your pores, let them crawl under your skin, and flood your flesh and bones. Throb to their rhythm and sway to their melody. Unresisted, their energy will incinerate the last remnants of judgment or doubt in your mind, the tension in your body, and, at last, themselves, leaving you light, clear, and warm.

Your beliefs, however, are fire-resistant. They are fixed, heavy, and rooted firmly. They stiffen your wings and stand in your way. You have to be very patient with them and with yourself when they upset you. Look each of them deep in the eye, and call them by their name. Explain to them that your trip is very personal, and your vehicle has no space for passengers. Say that it breaks your heart to leave them, yet it would break your back to carry them around. Only *you* can enter the next moment. When you are patient, they will loosen and fall on the side. Unburdened, you will meet no resistance on your Journey.

85

The Pen

[An Essential Exercise]

Do this exercise in steps, completing each instruction before moving on to the next. Remember, knowing is not enough. You need to *experience* to believe.

***

Place a pen about an arm's length away from where you sit.

Remember a wish about something you want to do, a wish you have been hatching for long, but have never brought to life for thinking that you could not do it.

Feel your wish as clearly and as deeply as you can, regardless of whether you can or cannot accomplish it. Feel your wish in your flesh and bone.

Now, remember your doubt. Remember it as clearly as you can.

What happens to your wish? Are you feeling it with the same intensity in your flesh and bone? If not, what do you feel in your body?

Look at the pen. Imagine that it is a magic stick . . . and you really-really want to have it . . . Imagine all you could accomplish with it . . . See yourself doing magic with its help, even making your wish come true . . . Feel the sense of *power* in your body.

Now, *move*: pick up your pen. Make sure you feel every portion of your move.

Was it difficult?

Did you doubt that you could do it?

If you did not doubt that you could do it, is it fair to assume you trusted yourself that you could pick up the pen, even if you did not verbalize it consciously?

How come you did not doubt yourself?

Was it *easy* to do?

Who made the judgment that it was easy to do?

Could it have been the one who, over the years, has told you what you could not accomplish?

The judger must have his or her reasons. Respect that. Never judge a judge.

Instead of arguing or contesting, let reality *rule*. You have just performed magic: you *did* what you really-really wanted.

Nut like Anybody Else

[A Lullaby]

Think of yourself as a nut. You sprout together with many thousands of your kind in the Big Round Forest. You love to play hide and seek, but as the years grow light becomes scant. Someone is always in your airways leaving very little stretching place for you. You hate crowded places where scrawny bystanders shed their parasites in your direction.

Then you get used to it. At least, you are not alone like that lonely, solitary oak on the hillside. From behind the ambush of your foliage, you watch him flirting with the sun. He is of your age, yet three times your size, with muscular branches, shiny leaves, and an irritatingly calm and easygoing attitude.

You become a philosopher and ponder about what really sustains you: the homey support of your environment, or what you are forced or willing to access from within you when you are left alone. Or is it both, and if so, to what extent?

After many years of anti-acid-inflammatory-biotic-depressant-anything-gulpable-therapy you decide, that strength from within your core is worth infinite times more than the support of others or their inanimate substitutes. Midlife crisis lends you the necessary courage and impulsiveness to pick up your roots. You exchange your family, and duties of providing oxygen, for a wild adventure in the tundra in hopes of meeting your *real* self. Your dream comes true ... with a sigh. He turns out to be just as scrawny as you were in the woods, and has the same attitude: anxious, often overwhelmed, irritable, and frustrated. After a quick, unemotional change of plans, you move back to the forest on a cold, rainy evening.

You renew your marriage vows to your doubt. You both gain weight. She gets bossier by the minute. She dictates your behavior and chains you to the constant, unremitting effects of the forest. When you rebel, in your lashing out, you cement your attachment to her. From then on you think twice and doubt twice ... as you dig for your roots again.

Exhausted, you drop your shovel and fall in your ditch, where you meet the Beast. She makes an offer you cannot refuse: she will make

88

your muscles strong, your leaves shiny and impeccable and your doubt content but there is a catch. Since you have nothing to lose you agree. She rattles her disclaimer: "Once you understand the process, you cannot claim ignorance!" You shake her hand . . . and walk away with an irritatingly calm and easygoing attitude.

She keeps her promise. You keep yours: every morning you wake up to *sense* the magic. *Your* magic.

What You Wish For

Of happiness you dream.
Joy, you practice.
When you doubt,
you practice helplessness and fear.
You practice, too, when you are unaware,
when you do what you did not want to do,
and in the very process you become unwanted.
If you do not practice what you wish for,
you will be an excuse and an obstacle.

The Fork

[An Essential Exercise]

Do this exercise standing. Bend your right arm at the elbow so that your forearm parallels the ground and points straight ahead of you. Make a fist, then release your index and middle finger, and keeping them together, stretch them out so that they become extensions of your forearm pointing ahead.

Place the tip of your left index finger on the back of your right hand, between the base knuckles of your right index finger and middle finger. Imagine that this is where you stand.

Move your left fingertip away from your body, down the groove created by the two right-hand fingers. Do it a few more times in the same direction. This is the path you go down day in and day out, propelled by your automatic thoughts and reactions.

Return your left fingertip to the dent between the knuckles on the back of your right hand.

Keeping your right index finger pointing straight ahead, slowly move your middle finger apart and create as wide a fork as you can.

Keeping your left fingertip between your right knuckles, look at the space you have created: instead of your convenient groove, which you were able to walk down on *even with your eyes closed*, now you are facing a cliff between two ridges. You have no choice but to choose one of them to get ahead.

Close the gap between your right fingers and redo the exercise, going down the groove a couple of times and then opening up the fork.

Notice how wedging space between your fingers creates alternative directions and forces you to make a conscious decision.

Which ridge will you choose: the one that points in the same (old) direction, or the one that leads in another?

Either option can work, as long as your eyes are open.

Guilty of Anger

She is a no-nonsense high-powered litigation lawyer.

I take a chance of enraging her by plainly stating my opinion: "There is nothing altruistic, nice, or appropriate about repressing *feeling* angry. If you do, it will, sooner than later, subconsciously influence your behavior. You will find yourself reactive, annoyed or in rage often toward others, not just the person you are angry with."

She stays calm.

"So why does the Bible say that I should show the other cheek to those who slap me in the face? Doesn't that mean that I should not feel angry, that I should repress those urges?" she asks as if to test me.

"Repress the acting out, not the urges," I reply bluntly. "Of course, there are as many interpretations of the Bible as people who read it, and I am no expert in religious studies. It seems to me, though, that holy scriptures of all faiths use words as metaphors to illustrate their point rather than to restrain access to self-support. Historically, however, institutions have at times interpreted the same words differently to preserve their power. If the Bible is important to you, you may need to decide for yourself how you want to understand it. But if, for example, "Repent!" is not meant to encourage you to feel your feelings and to recognize them as your own, how could you forgive yourself or others?"

She looks curious.

"What about guilt then?"

"Repression of feelings can certainly lead to it and in most cases it does. Do you feel guilty?"

"I often feel guilty just because I feel angry, for instance, toward my mother. I do not want to hurt her, she does not deserve it."

"Do your emotions feed on merits?"

She smiles, letting me know she understands my sarcasm.

"Nevertheless, it is important to respect how *you* feel, *now,*" I add.

"I do not respect myself when I feel angry."

"What does it make you feel about yourself?"

"It makes me feel like a failure," she admits.

I watch her travel somewhere far beyond me where I cannot accompany her any longer. I nod to acknowledge that I have heard her, in case she still sees me from the corner of her eyes. Then I sit quietly so that my words do not disturb her intimacy with herself, or distract her from feeling what she is ready to feel. A couple of minutes later her attention returns to the room and she looks straight at me. I take it as my cue to continue.

"Do you believe that your emotions can hurt your mother?

"Sometimes. Is that normal?"

"It is . . . especially around age four. It is called magical thinking. Some people carry it with them into adulthood."

"My mother says she hurts when I am angry with her."

I wait for a moment to make sure that she, too, heard the echoes of what she said.

"Are you certain she means your private feelings only known to you?"

She looks puzzled, so I put it differently.

"Is it 'how you feel' that erodes her and your self-respect, or rather 'what you do,' when you do not allow yourself to *feel*? In the latter case, could she have objected to your rude tone, reaction, attitude, or snide remarks spewed up by the *tension* of your fermenting repressed emotions?"

She is silent. So am I in order to stay out of her way as she digests what she may have understood. After a few moments, when she looks at me again, she appears open and inviting, so I decide to go to the next level.

"When you allow yourself to feel your emotions fully, in order to become so familiar with them that you understand where they come from and what they are about, you *wedge time* between an impulse and acting it out, allowing yourself to make conscious decisions. You *create* the *option* of not acting out."

"And if I do not allow myself to feel my emotions fully?"

"Then everything happens automatically, according to how you *learned* to react, even if it is damaging to you or others. You keep acting like a machine programmed by your parents' and their parents' heritage."

She soaks in every word I say as if she is gathering energy and courage to understand her predicament: Is she the one to have to start swimming against the current of her previous generations and to finally stop paying taxes on family guilt?

"My father used to yell or beat us when we made *him* angry. My mother could not listen to how I felt. It made *her* too anxious, I guess. She used to say: 'Come on, you do not really feel that way, do you?' Well, of course, I did not feel *that way*. It seems as if I just stopped feeling, so that I do not feel *that way*." She abruptly stops talking.

"Which way?" I venture.

She cannot respond, but her body does, wrung by resistance to surrendering to *feeling* what she wants to tell me. Then, suddenly, her tears decide to disobey her orders.

I have never seen her cry. Stoic as she is, she is used to lumping all emotions under a general, nonspecific term: frustration. I do not know if it is the first time that she is undefended, naked, exposed to *how it feels* to feel what her thoughts cannot tell her. I sit back. Instead of offering comfort by holding her with compassionate words, I simply hold the space around her in an attempt to protect her privacy from my thoughts. She soon comes to fetch me.

"Tell me more!" she urges me still sobbing.

"What do you feel?" I inquire.

"Sad."

"Is it okay to feel sad a little longer?"

She nods.

"Where do you feel the sadness in your body?"

"In my chest."

"What does it feel like?"

"Like wringing . . . churning."

"Is it okay to feel the wringing and the churning a little longer?"

"Yes."

"Close your eyes . . . take a deep, long breath, and let the wringing and the churning flood your whole chest, fill up every nook and infiltrate all the tissues . . . When you exhale, allow your feelings to percolate your cells . . . Breathe in the pain you feel and make sure you *feel* it in *every cell* of your body . . . then breathe out. Breathe it in, then out . . ."

To deepen relaxation, I guide her through *Induction* of whole-body sensation.

In a couple of minutes the muscles on her face relax, and her breathing becomes easy and regular.

"When you are ready, you can open your eyes."

She slowly opens her eyes.

"What do you feel?" I ask.

"Relaxed."

"Do you still feel wringing and churning in your chest?"

"No."

"What happened?"

"I do not know."

"That is a good start. What have you experienced?"

"First I felt the sadness, then the churning, then the more I felt the pain in my body the less it felt like pain."

94

"What did it feel like?"

"Like energy."

I pause to allow her to let what she has said sink in, then I continue.

"Was sensing your energy scary to you or uncomfortable?"

"No, quite the opposite . . . I felt energized."

I pause again.

"Do you still feel sad?"

"No... I am really not a sad type of person, you know..."

"Are you an angry type of person?"

"I would not say so, but I am more angry than sad, for sure."

"So what happened today?"

"I do not know . . . the sadness came out of the blue..."

"Where was it hiding all this time?"

She is pensive.

"Behind my anger, I am afraid . . ." she says finally.

"Behind your blue anger?"

She smiles in agreement. It is time for me to rest my case, but she is not ready to quit.

"So what shall I do when I feel guilty again?"

"What would you like to do?" I toss the ball back in her court.

"Shall I force myself to continue *feeling* guilty?"

"Have you forced yourself to feel sad during our session today?"

"No . . . not at all . . . there was no forcing . . . had I forced it, I probably would not have been able to feel anything . . ."

"That is possible."

"It felt like . . . I allowed myself to feel sad."

"So you can allow yourself to feel guilty to help you find the emotion it represses. And when you are ready to allow yourself to feel that *primary emotion* entirely, guilt will lose its purpose and repressive function and peel off you like an old, cracked skin."

Conflict

Go quietly into the conflict. Take many pauses and a long whiff, as you smell your way into it. Resist lashing out or blaming, because a chunk of your energy will depart with the words and the gestures.

Keep your ears, eyes, and mind open when you enter the conflict: remember that you are exploring a place you have always turned away from or could not avoid falling into. It may be scary and uncomfortable to consciously reexperience the helplessness you felt as a child, triggered by your current seemingly unrelated circumstances. Then, your parents were in charge and empowered, and they were "impossible". At least, that is how you felt. Nevertheless, each time someone does not see you or your truth now, or you fail to see theirs, you may still respond from the child's position: blaming others for what you feel.

Feeling hurt by them confirms their power and locks your focus in *their* reference point. That is why you feel out of control and act defensive: you are *not home* in your inner reference point. Anxiety or anger is the only logical result of hanging out in a foreign uncomfortable place. You argue their point aloud or *in your mind,* in order to avoid feeling. It is scary to recognize your hurt as yours, generated and nurtured only by you. First you lose your focus, and with that, control, then energy, then your mind.

Lashing out and blaming others for what they do, say, or think solidify the placement of your focus *outside* you: anger and fear are the strongest attachments. No wonder you feel outside yourself; you *are* outside yourself. When you blame yourself, you are still outside yourself, since your ego is only your self-image, a picture, a foreign object in your mind, not who you are, nor is it your home.

You are not what you *think*. You are what you *sense* in your body in this moment. The rest is fantasy. You are the pulsating, vibrating energy in your fingertips . . . stable, always at hand. You are life and life is your home.

Identify with the *energy* of your anger or fear, not with its *theme or content*. Let the burning and sizzling flood your body and recharge your batteries. It is your energy, which your cells worked hard to

96

generate. Let it empower you instead of your opponent's viewpoint. You need every bit of your energy to break your crusted, conditioned patterns of thinking and behavior, which deplete you. You need *your* energy to bring your point of reference *home*.

More Tools and Exercises

Symptoms

If you feel that all you have
is your symptoms,
then use them *all*
to teach you.

For if you get rid of your symptoms
before understanding them,
you get rid of your tools
to help you understand yourself.

Balance . . .

. . . is resonance.
It is everything
at once.
When you hurt,
you are imbalanced:
you exclude something,
someone, or
some part of your body
from your vision or
understanding.

Center

Imagine a line, between you and your opponents, as a diameter of a sphere. You are perched on one end; they nest on the opposite side. You arc so far removed from them that you can only see yourself, hear your own thoughts, and feel your own emotions.

Now, start moving slowly on the line towards the center, and leave your thoughts, emotions, and self-image gently tucked in at your end. You will know you have reached the midpoint when you understand your opponents' thoughts as well as your own, see *them* as clearly as you see yourself, and you realize how *they* feel.

In that moment, any anger you may harbor will disappear. It is hard to feel angry and empathic at the same time. Look around. You will see and understand the rest of the world at once. That is how you know you are in the center.

The center is the source of your energy as well as your opponents'. It is the place of resonance: amplitudes of frequencies that are close to each other will suddenly increase, just as in physics. Why not use universal laws to your advantage? Use your opponents' energy to amplify and recharge your batteries. They will use yours.

Going out on others' limbs, however, away from the center, and hearing their opinions louder than yours will cause just as much interference and decrease in your energy as isolating yourself in your niche.

Practice centeredness. When you are centered, you cannot but realize that half of your balance rests on what you oppose.

Freedom . . .

. . . is hidden
in your capacity
to adjust and accommodate.

Power

When you *feel* power,
you do not need to use it.

Caution

Those who are fearful
want power.
Those who are powerful
do not need an excuse
for having it.
Beware of those
who are fearful
and have an excuse
to use power.

. . . You Are . . .

.

.

.

i
n
v
i
s
i
b
l
e

energy.

If you choose to manifest,
accept to become vulnerable;
take responsibility for your fears,
impulses, and other distractions from . . .

Mastery

Practice does not make the master;
masters make practice their priority.

Dancing

Every moment is a train:
it takes you on a ride
or runs you over when you fight
its momentum.

But every moment
becomes a dancer
when you touch.

Swirling, you absorb
each other's scent in passing
as you roll off into the arms
of the next moment.

Treatments

Play . . .

. . . is the best matchmaker
between you and this moment.

Awareness

Play or pay.

Joy . . .

. . . is the skill of experiencing;
it is practice itself.

Moderation . . .

. . . is the single best treatment available.

Good Relationship

Make friends
with your emotions.

Patience . . .

. . . is the magic potion.

Faith

When all else fails,
something has to go;
everything will take its place.

Practice

Your
past and your future
will remain your thoughts;
reality is
what you practice.
This moment is your conscience:
it reflects what you
practice.

Homework and Options

Homework

1. Do not resist or avoid emotions. Always move toward and join them. They are your *allies and warriors*. Allow their energy to permeate you and clear your mind. If you act out, however, you leak energy through words and gestures, and you will stay frustrated, confused, or helpless.

2. Gradually extend the time you let yourself feel discomfort when emotions flare, until you recognize and *sense* fear or sorrow behind anxiety and anger. Hang on a little longer each time, and see where the process takes you. If you are patient, you will travel to the root of your emotions.

3. There, you have a choice to feel them as sensations, not as threats. *Identify with their energy, not with their content.*

4. When you feel resistance, scan for thoughts pushing you. Do not push back or argue. If you do, the increasing resistance will deplete you.

5. Practice *Induction* to clear your mind of noise and build self-support.

6. Always experience first, then do not explain. Aim for clarity, not reason.

7. Do not let words limit your comprehension or potential. Do not be seduced by knowledge or logic alone. *Use* thinking, do not be controlled by it. Let it *refine,* not confine, your experience. Aim for power, not its concept.

8. Do not show power or use force. *Be* empowered and use caution. Remember that you were, are, and will be what you practice.

9. Exercise your skills to *connect* with others through your inner reference point. Remind yourself that you understand what and whom you are ready to accept for the moment. Practice centeredness to maintain balance. *Then* make choices.

123

10. Participate in interactions with courage: You and the universe are One of which the "O" stands for "Other."

Options

I do not resist
          I feel
I do not avoid
          I inquire
I do not dread
          I connect
I do not talk
          I acknowledge my anxiety, then I communicate
I do not complain
          I adjust
I do not argue
          I listen
I do not express frustration or annoyance
          I notice my tendency to control
I do not lash out in anger
          I recognize my thoughts that blame
I do not engage myself with aggressive persons
          I move on
I do not take revenge
          I understand
I do not judge
          I explore
I do not blame
          I admit
I do not push
          I ask
I do not insist
          I review my goals
I do not convince
          I refocus on my inner reference point
I do not expect
          I act
I do not resent
          I feel grateful for the reminder
I do not lie
          I face my wish
I do not fail
          I learn
I do not despair

I take time to play
I do not indulge in excess
I rekindle my awareness
I do not tire
I rest
I do not ail
I care for my body and soul
I do not hurry
I prioritize
I do not help
I encourage
I do not give
I share
I do not teach
I practice
I do not seek recognition
I attend to my purpose
I do not know
I seek clarity

Appendices

Induction to Meditation

Do you believe that meditation is too difficult to learn or that it requires special circumstances and significant time, which your busy lifestyle cannot accommodate? If the answer is yes, these misconceptions may have prevented you from making use of a powerful tool to help you manage anxiety, anger, fatigue, depression, insecurity, and pain without side effects. Meditation is also applicable and effective in the process of learning, problem solving, and decision making.

There are different forms and traditions of meditation, but they all foster *experience* by means of bypassing thinking. The latter may seem impossoble to accomplish by compulsive "thinkers," people who think too much.

If you are one of those people, you are most likely a worrier, too. You probably complain about difficulties with "turning off" or "slowing down" your thoughts, or disengaging from them, all of which can worsen anxiety and mental fatigue. Since the biggest obstacle of learning meditation is addiction to thoughts, it is best to start with direct, simultaneous, sensory exercises as described step-by-step in *"Induction,"* (page 131).

Induction applies principles of neurophysiology, meditation, and self-hypnosis to *induce* deep relaxation with heightened alertness in a couple of minutes or even seconds, with practice. When applied correctly, it significantly relieves anxiety and increases processing capacity by reducing the rate of distracting, ineffective thoughts.

Induction is not so called positive thinking or trying to relax. Relaxation and optimism are two of its many beneficial results. *Induction* is a series of focusing exercises to foster whole-body experience and to reverse habitual mental dissociations from your body-sense. It improves your ability to suspend the restrictive or negative effects of thinking on your biological and psychological functions.

Induction is the *practice* of quickly and effectively switching focus from thoughts to sensations at will. When you practice induction, you disrupt mental ruminations, which engender inhibitions, anxiety, and irritability. While shifting from a disproportionately cognitive mode

129

(intellectualizing, trying to figure things out) to the more fundamental and balanced experiential one, you engage *all* your capacities to process information. By assigning a complimentary role to thinking instead of a leading one, you decrease the effects of cognitive errors on your body and mood without loosing awareness or your ability to problem-solve. To the contrary, with less anxiety, your capacity to appropriately respond to challenges increases.

None of the different levels of *Induction,* from basic to more advanced, require special skills or previous studies. Their success and effectiveness are based on and guaranteed by your own biology, any time you *practice.*

In summary, *Induction* is intentional self-energy-centeredness. It allows for a reliable way to short-circuit ineffective thinking, which worsens anxiety. *Induction* enhances a strong sense of self-support reproducible any time and at any place.

By decreasing mental inhibitions, *Induction* promotes direct access to your whole-body wisdom, tranquility, and sense of energy, which together form your *permanently* reliable support system . . . as long as you practice accessing them.

Induction

[Basic Level]

Carry out each instruction completely before moving on to the next. For the most benefit, do not turn the page until you have *experienced* the effects of the exercise.

Sit comfortably, leaning against the back of a chair . . . allow all the sounds to come very, very near you . . . if you are in a room and hear the ticking of a clock . . . if cars go by outside . . . or if the telephone rings . . . whatever you hear . . . let it all happen . . . and let the sounds come to you . . . to share the space.

Feel your fingertips without moving them . . . there is no need to look for anything special . . . just sense them . . . sense that they *are* . . . and what it feels like to have fingertips . . .

Now feel your toes . . . feel them from the inside out . . . sense what it is like to have toes . . . (if your toes are numb or cold, feel your feet)

Feel your fingertips . . . and your toes . . . *at the same time* . . .

When you feel them at the same time . . . follow this sensation from your toes all the way up your legs . . . through your pelvis and abdomen . . . through your chest . . . and throat . . . into your head . . . and feel your head . . .

Feel your head . . . fingertips . . . and toes . . . *all at the same time.*

If thoughts come by . . . let them be . . . wherever they are . . . keep all your doors and windows open so they can leave just as easy as they came . . .

Feel your head . . . fingertips . . . and toes . . . *at the same time* . . .

Notice, that in the moment you feel your head . . . fingertips . . . and toes . . . *at the same time* . . . you feel your body.

This is what it *feels* like to have a body . . . your body . . .

Your body *sensation* is your inner reference point . . . *this* is your reality in this moment . . .

Notice your experience . . .

***

If the rate of your thoughts was one hundred percent before *Induction,* what percent would you assign to it when you felt your head, fingertips, and toes *at the same time* during your exercise?

If there is no difference, accept it and redo the exercise sometime later today.

If you did not experience what you expected, notice your expectation and allow yourself to feel fully what you feel as a reaction to your disappointment.

If there is a difference, *feel and enjoy* it. Do not try to explain your *experience*.

Additional Information

If you would like to be guided by Dr. Ormos
through the original unabridged *Induction*
(basic, intermediate, and advanced levels)
or listen to this manual on CD,
visit the online store
at www.sobrasinstitute.com to order.

The website also provides information
on seminars and additional learning materials
as they become available.

Consultations for clinicians
can be scheduled by calling
(508) 540-2575.

To order materials by phone,
call (800) 345-6665.

Your questions or comments
via email to info@sobrasinstitute.com
will be appreciated and considered
when new materials are being prepared.